Build your own h

3rd book in the "Living in ~~Spain series~~

Intro

After living and working in Spain for 17 years David started on his dream to buy a plot of land and then design and build his own dream 4 bedroom house, with pool, workshops, gym and gardens, just as he wanted it.

This book takes you through every step of David's adventure, it really was an adventure, outlining the costs in detail and highlighting the hurdles he had to overcome while providing valuable tips and advice with links to companies and sites that will save you time, money and stress if you are planning a similar building or renovation project adventure in Spain.

After 25 years in the building industry and his years of building and renovation work in both Spain and the UK, David has shared his expert advice with others including his guest appearance on the BBC news channel and the Channel 4s " A place in the sun". He has appeared on Local radio stations and podcast interviews as well as providing help and info on all aspects of living and working in Spain on his own podcast show, blog, Facebook groups and YouTube channels.

This 2 yearlong adventure had its ups and downs and at the age of 59 David is still working on the almost finished house that he now enjoys with his Spanish wife in sunny Almeria.

These tips and advice are from years of experience working in Spain and dealing with the Spanish system and how to handle the mountains of sometimes unnecessary red tape and paperwork that's needed for such projects.

There are new strict building rules and regulations now in Spain that are difficult to navigate at times but David, with the help of his Spanish wife, who works for local government, will show that they can be less stressful if you have a heads up and are prepared beforehand.

"If you want what others have then you need to do what others do"

Following just some of David's advice will give you new insights and ideas on how you could make your house build or renovation go faster and easier with less stress, for less money.

There are some very valuable building insights with links to places, companies and trades people that are all over Spain where you can buy materials and contract workers at the best prices possible.

Many building projects in Spain run over budget and fall into problems or fail due to lack of experience, funds or planning. David has seen first-hand many British start similar projects of different sizes here in Spain and what they have done or didn't do to make it work.

If you want to build your dream house or just renovate a property in Spain, then this book will provide you with advice that will encourage you and guide you over hurdles that you would not have thought about if you have not already been through this adventure.

About the author

David was born in Brighton, England in 1962 and moved to Spain with his first wife but after 17 years of marriage and 3 years after moving to Spain David divorced and started a new life in Almeria on the south coast of Spain his own.

After a few years David met and married Llani a Spanish girl who has helped him in all aspects of the build including getting dirty and mixing cement and laying bricks.

After improving his Spanish David worked for both English and Spanish clients as well as several other nationalities in Spain building and renovating properties all over Spain.

Originally trained as a cabinet maker, David worked in the building industry as a carpenter in Brighton and later as maintenance manager on Brighton Pier for several year, a job he loved all except the bad weather.

A long with David's carpentry jobs, David run 2 karate clubs after gaining his black belt and for 2 years was a full time karate instructor in Brighton and self-defence teacher managing 2 local clubs of his own.

Paragliding was his passion and he gained pilot rating and continued paraglide in Spain for the first few years, enjoying better flying conditions then he had experienced in the UK.

Travel is also David's passion and he has travelled extensively all over Europe and America but his dream holiday was just a few years ago when he had 3 weeks in Bora Bora, staying in a high end over water bungalow costing 900 dollars a night in the middle of the south pacific.

Being now married to a Spanish wife David has travelled all over Spain using his wife as a personal guide, enjoying most of the top cities and towns in Spain. Although English David now feels his sole is Spanish.

Seeing many people fail or give up on their dreams, David now tries to help and encourage others by sharing his tips, help and advice through his online sites and books.

David has not let his dyslexia hold him back from writing 3 books or running his blog and although criticised on his spelling, feels it more important to get the information out there even though he does try to get it right with the help of siri or auto correct.

David's long term plans are to just potter about on his new house whether it is in his garden or allotment he has created or relaxing in his personal gym or private pool.

Most of his friends are now Spanish and David enjoys nothing better than entertaining these friends at his new dream house in Spain. Most weekends David and friends can be found enjoying a cold beer in the pool or just sitting on his terrace chatting over tapas.

The information was not readily available to David when he made his move to Spain and for this reason David has created his sites on social media and these books to not only provide first-hand information but encouragement to those who really want a better way of life.

Table of Contents

Chapter 1

Why build my own House in Spain

Who hasn't dreamed of building their own dream house in the sun some day when they win the lottery?

It was always a dream of mine but that dream stayed in the back of my mind for many years until the time was right for me to get it started.

It is actually easier to start then you think but it's not until you start that you see the tremendous hill you must climb.

In the 19 years I have lived in Spain, I have bought and sold several properties here including apartments and I have also rented properties to live in myself and to rent out to others for an income.

My first property here was rented and this is something I strongly suggest others do even if they feel the need to buy out right from the start.

Personally I wanted to buy but was told by a bank manager here to rent first to see if I really liked that area and as there are many taxes to pay on buying and selling in Spain, this was good advice.

So renting is what I did in what I thought was a great area very near a beautiful beach, one morning after a few months of living in that property, we were awoken to crashing and banging of plates from a local hotel just behind where we were renting.

This had not been a problem until then as it was not the height of the summer season but this morning the weather was warm and sunny and the kitchen staff had the windows open and we could hear all the crashing and banging.

At this time I needed to get up early for work but it was still earlier than I planned and was very annoying for weeks on end.

So glad we didn't buy in that area and later found a 2 bed apartment just 10 mins up the road in a quieter area but still within walking distance to all we needed.

After my divorce I lived along for some time in my house that was 4 bedrooms and too big for me alone and became difficult to maintain financially so was forced to sell and move in with Llani who was then my new girlfriend of about 6 months.

Llani lived after her divorce, with her daughter Marta who was just finishing university aged about 25.

The apartment Llani had was newly renovated and updated by llani and her interior designer.

LLani had spent a lot of money on totally renovating the place after her divorce and it was perfect. The views from the terrace where amazing over the community pool and the sea in the distance. One of the reasons I personally loved living there was that there were many great FREE tapas bars all within walking distance and we would go out for tapas more than 3 times a week.

This 3 bedrooms and 2 bathroom apartment was in an apartment block, just 10 mins walk to amazing beaches and 2 mins to great Tapas bars. This apartment had a community pool and gardens that were all very nice and we all lived there very happily for around 5 years.

The main problem with living in Apartments anywhere in the world is that they are really only as good as the neighbours you live with.

This turned out to be the main reason we built our own house.

Our apartment was about 20 years old and seemed well built but the walls were not very well insulated and that meant we could hear people above below and each side of us.

To start with we our neighbours were very nice as they mostly kept to themselves and as they worked we didn't see or hear much of them.

Then it started.

First the people living below us rented out their apartment to a young couple with a son aged about 10. He kicked a football against the walls a lot and at weekends the guy would play loud music till late into the night.

The working guy next door moved away and rented out his place to a young working mum with a 6 year old daughter that cried a lot. This young mum would skype her mum who lived in South America and we could hear all their conversation that lasted for hours about 3 times a week.

Then on the other side we had an old guy who snored a lot and as the walls were so badly insulated it became a nightmare,

Around this time my Brother who was also from Brighton was very interested in finding a holiday home here near us so as he could one day retire here, Remember this was before Brexit and before we had any idea of all the changes that were about to come into effect.

So we started looking at places with my brother who was coming here almost every 2 months for a week and getting an idea of what he could get for his money.

On one house inspection we had with him, we found a really nice house not far from where we lived and it seemed perfect for him.

It was one on his top list to maybe go for on his next visit and really gave him food for thought. My brother returned to England to think about his options and it started Llani and I talking about how places like that would suit us. At first it was a bit of a joke as it was not really where we wanted but the house seemed very nice, although it needed a few updates that I was more than capable of doing.

This is what really started us on our own house hunting trips to just start seeing what was out there that we could afford and may like to move to.

After several weeks of not seeing what we wanted I turned to my wife and half-jokingly said that I could build a new house for the same price. To my surprise she responded ok let's do it.

This is when we found a good estate agent that we liked who was a very well dressed, very keen young guy who had just started with a new partner in a small estate agents business they ran together.

This agent is who found us several plots to view and put us in touch with the one we finally bought through him.

Buying a new house is great but it's never really just as you want it and even if it's close you still need to do some improvements or adjustments to make it yours and this costs money and time. Often they are not really in the right place or facing in the wrong direction and all of this you can have total control over if you build your own house.

Not only that but for me making things with my own hands and any DIY projects I love doing but this, building your own dream house in Spain, was the panicle and if I didn't go for it now then I would probably be too old and never do it.

Risky? Yes but what's not nowadays, even crossing the road or walking the streets without a bloody mask can kill you so personally I feel dreams are for going after full speed and if they fail it's not from lack of trying.

So many people thought we were mad, crazy or stupid and maybe they were right but now many of them are enjoying a swim in our private pool in my private garden, at my private house.

At the age of 55 I have lived in some nice homes and both small and large but each time we moved it was to make our lives more comfortable than before but now this was to be the last ever move and last ever house so we needed to make it just how we wanted, so with years of living in houses and homes that were ok, this one was going to be perfect.

The idea was also to never need to go out if we didn't want to like bars restaurants and gyms.

Our new house would have a gym, pool and a bar, a swim up bar at that as well as my own allotment and workshops, so there should be no need for us to want to go anywhere except the local supermarket.

As we get older I guess the need or want to go out reduces as it gets to be harder to drive or park where you like so why not try and have it all right where you want it, At home.

Thousands of people dream of building their own house but most don't because they think it's too hard and well yes its hard but I feel you get out of life what you put in and this will be not just a house build but the biggest adventure of our lives.

For me personally it was also a need to build my own as we had just about had enough of noisy neighbours and although we loved living in that area at the time and would probably been happy there many years we just sort of outgrow it. Now being married to a Spanish Girl I really got to enjoy the Spanish way and that meant a lot of entertaining in their homes and ours and our apartment was just not as big as we wanted.

After looking at many other properties, both new and old, with the idea to do up or renovate, this was almost the road we took but really the only thing that stopped us here was location on what we did look at and there just was nothing we found in the area we liked enough to go the renovation road.

So we took the plunge and decided to just build exactly what we needed. A more expensive road that's for sure but we just go so few up with looking they we made the jump.

Looking back maybe we should have looked at more but after you have seen about 20 you start to get fed up. With a new build we feel that the area is right and when the house is finished it will have more value but the problem here is that we now don't want to sell as it's our perfect home so whatever the offer unless it was millions I don't think we will ever sell it especially with all the hard work that we have put into it.

Renovating in the right area is a great idea if your planning on selling it on later but again its all down to area really to get the best price.

Chapter 2

What kind of house are we building?

Here I will try and layout what we are building and how we think it will look but if you pop over to my blog there are all the plans videos and photos for all to see. http://britishexpatsinspain.com/davids-dream-house-in-spain

Being English I did have an idea of what type of house I wanted to build and in what style but remember I am now also married to a Spanish girl who has had a different upbringing and lived in different styles of houses and apartments.

Both of us wanted similar things luckily enough and Llani loved the English style of houses with their nice gardens that you don't really see much of here, especially here in Almeria where it's just easier to tile all the garden areas due to the very dry weather here all year round.

Llani has 2 children, both grown up with one living away and the other about to fly the nest and work away. We didn't really need a big house but wanted to have 4 bedrooms and an office. Llani had been working from home occasionally and with the covid thing now here to stay we feel she will be working from home more in the future so an office were we can keep the computers and have a place to go away from the rest of the house was important.

There are some parts of the house that are really English like the big solid wooden front door that I handmade from local hardwoods all jointed that has some resemblance to an English castle door and that was no coincidence.

The wooden looking wall panels in the lounge and hall ways are also what I am use to seeing in some older English manor houses that we both really like.

The office will at a later date be all wood panelled as well to look like a real old English gentlemen's office. This will be a project for me at a later stage.

Below I have included some photos of the house but all updated photos and videos can be seen on my blog. Links are at the end of the book.

Below is the still not finished view from the front

View from back Garden

Finding work in Spain

I have always said that there is loads of work in Spain but it's just that many don't go that extra mile and try hard enough or train to get the skills that are needed.

After staying in an old castle in Scotland some years ago Llani wanted a big fireplace so this was as big as we could find here and its great in the winter months.

That's the flue pipe next to me and I did have to climb up the 7m high chimney breast to fit it all. We don't really get that cold a nights here in Almeria but around November and December we like to get it going as it just feels and looks so great.

That's when my climbing skills and equipment came in handy.

So the house build would be 235sm house on a 800sm plot of land and an underground garage of 200sm, total build area is 435 sm plus the pool bar 3m x 4m. The garage would have a space for 1 car and my motorbike, a gym, separate store room for all the junk and the rest for me to use as a workshop where I will be building all the furniture and doors, plus the general daily house build projects.

Below are some plans of the house. There were some adjustments to these plans but not much. The bathroom in the garage was not needed and it saved us 3000 taking it out as there is a bathroom tax here on new builds so 2 bathrooms is we feel enough.

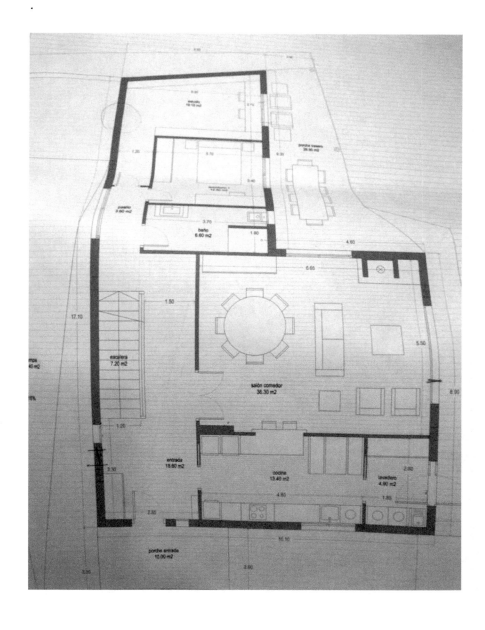

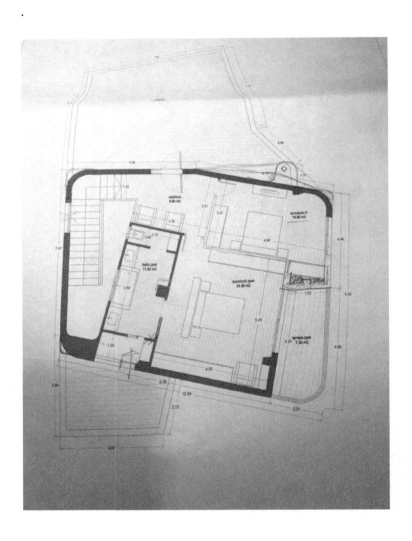

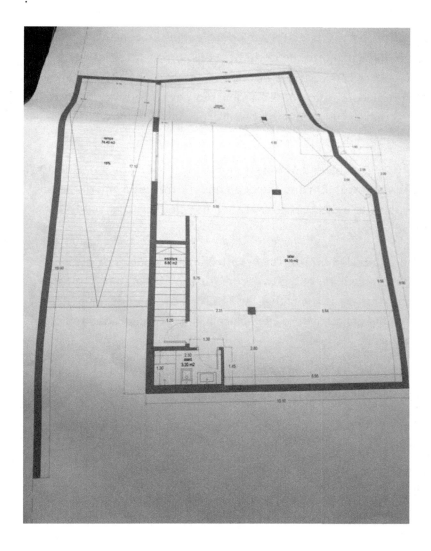

On the ground floor would be the entrance hall area of 3m x 3m and a staircase with decorative iron railings and wooden handrail on top, going up to the first floor. Staying on the ground floor is the kitchen with built in breakfast bar seating at the table for 5 people and at the end of the kitchen a utility room with all the washing and drying appliances and a door leading out onto the back paved patio and cloths drying area.

From the entrance hall 2 large French doors leading into the lounge 8m x 6m and a serving hatch into the kitchen. In the corner of the lounge a large open real fire with seating in front and a large TV on the wall above. Beside the fireplace 2 patio doors opening out onto a Terrance of 9m x 3m with direct access to the garden that is all artificially grasses with a side tiled pathway leading to the back allotment area and pool.

The pool situated at the end of the garden being 9m long by 4m wide and 1m at shallow end with 2m and the deep end. At the deep end of the pool is a ramp leading to a tiled bench seat for 6 people that faces out to the swim up pool bar.

The allotment is walled off from view with 2 arched doors, one at each end and is where I will try and grow some fruit and vegetables. At the end of the allotment there is a wall that I will make a cut out and have access to the roof of the garage where I will place a large wooden shed to house garden furniture.

We have also built a brick BBQ near the pool and already used to this year entertaining our friends here.

 At the front of the house as you drive through the electric sliding gates to the right will be a covered car port to house 2 cars and my motorbike and this would be made from wood with a covered top as shade.

The exterior of the house is all constructed in the latest thermic brick with a 50mm geo thermic insulation and then 13mm plasterboard internal walls.

The outside face of the house is finished off with 2cm of white capa fina, that's the Spanish plaster here that we then painted brilliant white.

All bedroom floors are wood laminate floors and all the other floors throughout are tiled with porcelain tiles including the stairs and kitchen work tops that are also porcelain. All tiling was done by me except the kitchen worktops as they were cut especially and fitted by a local company that specialises in porcelain.

The property is surrounded by a 2m high white blockwork wall and the front garden to the street has a 60mm high wall with iron railings on top at also 2m in height. Sliding electric gates of 3m for the drive entrance and an iron gate for pedestrian entrance with a touch pad coded entry and video door entry system.

Only 1 key and that's for the main front door of the house, all other doors open in with no locks from the outside, the front gate can be opened by touch code or with your mobile phone but the main front door is 1 security key.

What's the area like?

The plot is near Almeria main international airport and by car its 6mins drive from our new house. We don't get any noise from the planes but do get the odd plane fly over depending on the direction of the wind but the airport is closed at 10pm every night.

We have 3 hotels on the coast road in front of the beaches and shops with a few nice bars and cafe's. All this just 2 mins drive from the house so that's close enough to be handy and far away enough to not bother us.

Our Street is one of just 4 new streets that were built in the middle of a private golf course and the 4 streets are part of a gated community where we have private roaming security patrols and Private Street cleaning services with all the houses being no more than 10 years old.

As the streets are private there is no public traffic so very quiet roads indeed and there are no rubbish collections as we have bins places at the ends of each street where you place your rubbish and it is vacuumed down under the road and away as soon as you drop it in so no mess and no need to collection drivers.

Tapas are a big thing in Almeria as you may know if you have been following me and I do like my tapas. Here In this part of Almeria tapas are free to order off the menu and cooked fresh if you have a beer or wine, so we have tapas bars near us that we go to often with friends and family and this is another reason why we love this area so much.

Beaches all around this area are pretty good being sandy and very clean but just 15 mins drive from our new house is Caba de Gata which is famous for its award winning beaches and natural park lands and is a place where many Spanish go at weekends to chill out and enjoy the sea.

The beaches just 2 mins from our new house have a mixture sand and gravel but pretty nice and have some lovely bars that do free tapas and you know David loves hid Free Tapas.

Remember of course that Tapas are free in this part of Almeria and yet another reason why I wanted to build in this area of Almeria.

One other reason is the weather and I know people say that it's not all about the weather but that's the ones that don't get sun all year round. Even in December we can if we wish sunbath on the beach during the day.

Working in Brighton in November at 3.30pm it would be dark wet and bloody cold but here at the same time I can still be working outside in a T shirt during the day and at night it's never that cold to need a large coat like the UK but maybe a light jacket or jumper.

Chapter 3

Choosing the right plot of land

Not as simple as you may think here as there are plots that may look great and also be in a great area but we needed to check the ground and just what we could and could noit build in that area as all have very different rules as to what you can do.

We had an idea of where we wanted to be but like most things it came down to money, as our first choice was right near the beach but that was just crazy prices even though we did look at one or 2.

I had lived in Roquetas del mar and Aguadulce plus a few areas near to Almeria airport, both in apartments and houses including a new 4 bed house about 15 mins drive from the beach that suited me very well right up until my divorce, after that I had to sell it to pay off my ex-wife.

Although I liked these places they started to become touristy and I wanted to be elsewhere and had seen some lovely plots of land along the coast road that would be perfect but as we later found out the prices for the land alone were out of this world.

We both love the beach but knew that with tourists in summer months it was best to be slightly back from the coast for a quieter life.

The new estate agent guy we found suggested that we get our apartment valuated to help give us an idea of our budget. Once he had seen it and he had given us a price range we put it up for sale with him and he started looking for land for us.

We also looked at older properties that we could knock down and build on the land if they were in the right place for the right money.

One house we found in an area we really loved was perfect. Well the Land was but the house was very old and not at all in good condition. We were taken round by another agent working for the old lady who lived there. We were polite as we toured the house with the agent and the lady owner but it really was not a nice house.

The land it sat on was 1000sm and had a big wall around it with 2 large out buildings that would have been great as workshops and storage after we knocked down the house and started building our new house.

As my wife worked for local government she knew a girl who worked in the planning office and asked her about the area. She told my wife to go ask the planning officer.

Here's one of my most valuable tips.

Anyone can go to their local planning office and ask for free about any property they are interested in; if you get the plot number or address of the property they can tell you everything about that property.

We got the plot number from the estate agent although the address would have been sufficient. With the address or plot number you go to the planning office and ask to speak to the planning registry officer, I recommend taking a Spanish speaking friend if your Spanish is not up to par.

If you're not sure where this office is, just ask at your local town hall.

So once in, you tell the planning officer that you are very interested in buying that property and would like to know about it. In our first trip we met this planning officer who was very nice and after we provided him with the plot number. He found this very big book and started going through it until he came across the plot we were interested in.

It showed the house on that land and had dates and permissions all related to that house. The Owner's names and everything related to that property

We asked about the garages and he said that the plans showed no garages and no wall around the property. He told us that the owners had never asked for permissions for the garages or walls and that was not really a big problem as the owner could ask for permissions even now.

One very good contact I had made here over the years has his own business here and has lawyers working for him. He owed me a favour so I asked him if he could advise me on this situation.

He responded that if the owner had not got permission for the garage and walls that it was possible that they would need to pay a large fine or even take it all down.

No problem for us as we wanted to knock it all down anyway but he replied that yes it was a big problem as the notary would not let the sale go through as the papers were not in order.

We went back to the estate agents and told them what we had found out about the property, they were very surprised at our knowledge and said no worries the owner would sort all that out at the notary. The agent said that if we put down a deposit of around 2000 euros that week we could start things rolling. We knew this was not the case so backed away from the property.

Then the perfect land came up, well we thought it was.

One of my wife's work friends told us about it and gave us the owner's number who we arranged a viewing.

It seemed perfect. It was 1000sm nice and square on a corner in a very quiet area, only 10 mins from the beach. We also knew a girl from my wife's works who lived in the same street so visited her and saw around her house and had coffee with her and liked the area even more. This was it we thought.

The owner was a young guy about 35 who had inherited the land from his dead father. He wanted 90k for it. After a bit of research we found out that it was worth more around 70k so we offered 70k and this was turned down straight away. A few days later he called and asked us to meet for coffee near the land.

We seemed to get on well and thought this was it and that we were about to buy our land but he insisted that the land was worth 90k and would not move at all on his price.

At this time we had found a new architect that we liked called Jose. We had just met Jose and had told him about our plans and that we had found a plot of land, We arranged for him to meet us there and straight away he told us that was not a great area as property there was very slow in moving as the land behind was agricultural and had plans for new buildings and roads to be built in the coming months.

This put us off and he also explained that if we bought that land and built our dream house there it would not go up in value as the surrounding properties were all older and that would hold back our houses value.

Jose told us about this newish area near the airport that he had seen that was very new had great houses and was very sort after with just a few plots left.

That day we decided to go check it out on our own and as soon as we turned off the main road into the street we knew this was it.

The area was 5 mins drive from Almeria airport and only 2 mins drive from lovely beaches and had loads of small shops and supermarkets.

The plots we were looking at were all situated in just 4 streets that were in the middle of a golf course. It was on a gated community with private security and private street cleaners and services.

All very nice and all plots 800sm with block paved roads instead of tarmacked roads and tree lined streets.

The only problem was that these plots were 50k more than we wanted to pay, around 150k a plot.

Our agent called us that day to say he had a possible buyer for our apartment so we arrange a viewing that week, we had several very interested people but no takers.

After several viewings on our apartment we did find a buyer who offered us what we wanted and the sell started to move forward. Our agent also called us to say that he had a seller who had land where we had seen this dream plot and that we should go see it with him.

Just 2 days later we did and it was right in the same street as our architect had told us. It was perfect and the price was 150k.

The agent who was working for this Spanish seller was also working for us selling our apartment but he told us he could maybe get the guy down a bit,

That afternoon the agent called to say the price was 148k.

We told him yes as soon as our apartment sale was signed we would buy this land for 148k.

Just 3 weeks later our apartment deal was ready to sign and so we told the agent that we were ready to put a deposit on the land. They were asking for 2500 euros deposit, that was normal here then and so all was set for us to sign at the estate agents office that week.

Here in Spain once you put down a deposit it's not refundable if you pull out but if the seller pulls out then they have to give you double the deposit back. So the more deposit you put down the harder for the seller to pull out.

The day came and we went to the estate agents office to pay the deposit. As we entered the office and saw the agent we knew something was not right by the look on his face. He told us that the seller now wanted 5k more. We asked why and he said that he had found out that I was English and said they can go more.

We pulled out as it really was at out limit and I was not happy with dealing with people like that.

As we were leaving the agent told us that there was another plot of land just behind the one we had seen but it was owned by the seller's sister as she and her brother had been left the plots by relatives.

I told him that as soon as the sister found out what had happened she would want more as well. The agent told us that he would see what he could do.

The agent got back to us a few days later and told us that she had said ok at 148k.

We told the agent that we would only go through with it if she met us and signed for the deposit in 2 days' time or we would look elsewhere.

To our surprise she agreed and we signed for the land that week for 148k with a 3000 euro deposit paid.

Me driving one of the machines and moving some dirt.

Here is more concreate going into the underground garage.

Just look at all that re enforcing bar that is in the ground.

Here in this photo is the roof of the underground garage being poured.

That's the entrance ramp to the left that leads into the underground garage at the end of the ramp and to the right.

In the background you can see the shipping container that I had on hire that we used to keep all the materials and tools on site.

Concreate blocks and rebar supported by wood and acros below that came out after 3 weeks of drying time.

In this photo above, you can see just how many acros are needed to support each floor and the walls. They normally stay in position for 3 weeks to allow concreate to dry out well but we did leave some a little longer.

This way of construction here in Spain is much faster and none of the exterior or interior walls are load barring so you can design the house with more of an open plan. When planning the house I did try and think of where these needed to be so as not to be in the way of walls and living spaces once I had started to erect the internal walls of the house and there was really only one that I got wrong and that was in our on suit bathroom. Later I needed to move a wall about 200mm to accommodate my error so not bad really in the long run.

Chapter 4

Contracting architects and builders

Meeting architects and builders or trades people who will be helping you build your new home can be difficult in 2 ways.

First is how well do you get on with them? Like meeting anyone for the first time it's important that you click or at least feel you're on the same wave length.

Even this is not always enough though as you may like them very much and get on well but remember you want them to work for you so what is their work like.

A recommendation is always the best way to go and after you have sat down and had a little chat about your future plans, it's important to see just what they can do and to what standard.

Any good builder or architect will be more than happy to show you previous work and jobs that they have done or been involved in, it's the ones that don't want to show you are the ones to avoid.

You can easily check these people out and spending a little time doing this can pay dividends later. With architects just go to the collage of architects and ask them there what projects these people have done as its all recorded and registered and free to public viewing.

One architect that was recommended to us from a friend of my wife's but at the very first meeting I knew he was not for us.

He was about 50 years old and seemed nice at first but as I started to chat with him about what we had in mind, he seemed to be pushing us into his ideas and suggestions

That were very different to what we had in mind. The second one turned up 20 mins late and that's was a big red flag for me.

If you have an appointment with a new client who could be paying you 16k then you need to be on time.

Then we finally went with the 3rd one. Jose who was recommended to us by a friend and he was very nice we got on well right from the start and for me importantly he understood that I wanted to design everything but was happy for his input and suggestions.

Above the first Sketchup design I did. It changed a bit after that though.

For me it was important to get an architect that I would get on with as it was going to be a 2 year project and I didn't want us to have personality clashes.

Also you need a structural architect as well and this is a different person who really mostly gets involved with the initial build. For this we went with one that Jose worked with in his office and she was a lady who we met and found to be ok.

All the costs I will put in the costs chapter.

The next photo shows Just some of the cables for the ground floor electrics, so you can see why I needed some help running in these cables.

One thing I will say here about the structural architect is they often want to go over the top with things like concrete and blocks and beams

For example

On day 5 of the build after they had dug out the ground she called to say that the ground was not as hard as they thought and that we needed to put down 8 lorry loads of gravel before we started the footings pour. This would have been about 200 euros a lorry. I did some checks myself online and asked Jose what he thought. He did think it may be a lot and called her.

She told me that we needed at least 50mm of this gravel so we went with the minimum. That was 2 lorry loads Not 8 so a big saving. Remember that the ground was 4m deep dig out as that was the underground garage and then they would lay a clean concrete area of 50mm concrete all over that dirt just to walk on and peg out the lines. Then they would lay 450mm of reinforced concreate and rebar on top, so that was not going anywhere.

Also as we live in what they call an earthquake risk area, there are new rules here that means new house builds need stronger rebar in the piles and floors and ceilings plus the concreate is a harder mix so that gravel underneath will not have much effect on anything.

Then there were the double concreate beams she wanted us to put above each door and window to support the brickwork above. In the UK this is important as these beams take loads from the walls and floors above but here in Spain with the structure we have this is different, as the floors and ceilings are all supported by the pillars and the re enforced floors and rebar. The 3 courses of brickwork above each window or door only needs one beam as there is only about 9 bricks above it that the beam is supporting.

We saved several hundred by only having one beam above each door and window and the only difference is that I needed to fill in the difference with cement that is way cheaper than these concreate beams.

She means well and it was normal practices here but not necessary structurally.

Remember all photos and videos of this on my blog.
http://britishexpatsinspain.com/davids-dream-house-in-spain.

Now for the builders

One of the reasons we contracted Jose the architect was that he
was part of a family business and his brother was a builder for
larger new house builds all working from the same offices in
Almeria.

We thought it a great idea to keep them all together then if any
problems they can work it out between them and it would be more
in there interest to help each other as they are brothers.

The builders where Jose's Brother Juan, his crew of about 8 guys, all
Spanish who would be working on the structure of the house for
around 3 months and I would then be doing everything else myself.
Yes everything really.

I had also a plumber who I had known and worked with here for
several years and he was going to show me what pipes to put in and
where but I would be laying everything and he would just come and
make all the connections. Our plumber would be doing a lot of the
work for cost as he had been given some big contracts of work by
me in the past and it was a bit of a thankyou but still I would be
helping him each time he was on site and doing as much of his work
as possible under his guidance.

Many times he would start me off on a job and go do his work nearby at a client's house, then pop back now and then to check up on me.

For the electrics we contracted a guy, another Juan, we never knew him before but he was recommended to us from the plumber who we knew well and after meeting Juan and getting his quote we agreed he was the man for the job. Honestly we thought his prices a bit expensive but after the plumber chatted with us we decided to go with Juan.

Again here with the electrics the electrician and his crew would come help me mark walls and areas where I wanted plugs and switches and I laid almost all tubing for electrics and they did all the connections after.

So now we had the architect and builders all set.

In the beginning I wanted to contract 1 labourer to help me for the entire build but found it really hard getting anyone right.

At the start of the build I had arranged for 4 labourers to come meet me at the plot of land for an interview for the work.

Now I sent all 4 of these guys the address and my phone number after talking to them on the phone. All Spanish and all local to Almeria, all of them had been recommended to me.

So I had arranged interviews for 8,9,10 and 11 am that Monday.

On that morning at 8.30 no show and at 9.15 the second guy turned up. He turned up with a coffee in one hand and his breakfast in the other. I asked why he was late and he casually looked at his watch and said "More or less" I was not happy with his attitude. We chatted and he told me how he could do everything and how great he was and when I asked what he was doing last week he told me he had not worked for the last month as things where a bit slow.

Next at 10.20 the 3rd guy showed up and again I asked why he was late. He explained he was here but thought it was the house behind and drove around a few time to be sure. Anyway didn't like him either and after we chatted I said I would let him know.

Last of all was the 11am interview. On time but there was 2 of them. I was surprised and asked who they were. The older one about 60 said he was the boss and that the younger one would be working for him. I was still shocked I wanted a labourer and explained this. The older guy told me that's fine just pay him and he would pay the younger guy each week after he had worked for me.

I didn't like that strange arrangement and again told them I would let them know but never did,

The next day at 8.30 I saw a guy near the front gates laving at me. He told me he was here for the interview. It was the guy from 8am the day before that never showed up.

He told me he had to take his wife to work as her car was getting repaired and that's why he couldn't make it yesterday. I asked him why he didn't call me and he responded that he lost my number.

That night I told my wife that I was fed up with these people and that I will do it all my bloody self and she said ok I will help. At that time I thought she may be able to pass me the odd brick or maybe clean up after me now and then but later was very shocked at just how much she was able to do and how fast she learned.

Really she was better than most labourers as she knew nothing and everything she learned was from me and how I wanted it done, so no real conflict ever. That was until nearer the end of the build when she became an expert on mixing cement in the mixer and told me I was not to touch her mixer as I made it dirty.

Really though Llani was a very hard worker and I am so glad she helped me rather than those idiots who I know would have let me down.

Llanis first days she could not lift a bag of cement without a struggle and moving the mixer was out of the question but a few months in and she did all that completely on her own.

She stopped going to the gym as she said this was way better.

One day we had a delivery of a pallet of cement. About 60 bags and they put it in front of the gates and that was going to be in our way so as I was out getting materials Llani unloaded every bag to a new position all by herself before I got back.

The outside face of the house was capa fina blanco. That's a white cement plaster that goes on all the exterior walls and it's normally about 2cm thick. For this I contracted a company that originally said they would spray it on and have 3 guys do it in 2 weeks.

We agreed a price and they were set to start once the walls were all up.

So this company that we thought were great and got on well with at our meeting and when they started but it soon went downhill fast once they turned up to get started .

We had a bad start with them and I got shot of them but they had one guy who was a good worker who I later contracted on his own and as he was working illegally here then I paid his self-employment and insurance for 3 months so as he could work for me all above board. More on that later on in the book, it is a bit of a story and we did find a way that both of us did well out of it.

There is always a solution if you just look hard enough and that I had to do many times on this project.

Chapter 5

Financing the build

How did we get the money? Well my wife Llani sold her apartment and all the furniture and I had sold my house a few years before and my small business. It was all still not enough really especially as we went for the plot in the better area,

But it was enough to get a good start and we planned that Llani would continue working and use her money as I will be working full time 7 days a week on the build so saving labour costs.

We still needed a pretty big mortgage though that we hoped to pay off faster if possible.

Getting the mortgage was not easy as we were turned down by our own bank and the first 3 others we went to but found a new bank that asked us to change to them and have everything including all out bills go through them. We did this as I have never had any feelings towards any bank except that they are a business trying to get what they can out of you so we use them as must as we can as they use us and our money.

A few months after we had finished the house we bumped into our bank manager in the street in town and he told us that we were the last ones that his bank had given a mortgage to build a new house as the banks were getting tighter with lending money for these new builds as many people could not meet the deadlines and some had lost everything in not meeting these deadlines and the bank had taken the unfinished build that they didn't really want.

There are banks still lending for new builds as I know others who are doing it but you may need to put more down now of have very good plans and timings on the build. The bank wanted us to put down on paper 18 months for total build but we knew they had a maximum of 2 years so we went for that and did it just in 2 years. It's not completely finished yet but technically it is and we have all the correct papers but I still have a lot of decorating and finishing off to do.

My tip here is give yourself as long as you can, personally I would have liked to say 3 years, I know that sounds a long time but trust me working 7 days a week that fly's by.

We didn't go out for months before the build to save money and we didn't go out all through the build only maybe 2 or 3 times for a quick tapa but cheap as possible as all our money was needed for the build.

One thing I would say, try and get the bank to put on paper that your money goes into your account without them needed to do inspection visits or if they do get them to put on paper that you will not have to pay for these visits as we did even though they first said it was the bank that would pay.

We ended up paying over 1250 euros just to get them to give us our own money and also the stress of meeting these deadlines was not nice. Even then we had to wait another week after the visit to get that money put into our bank and remember we paid them for this 1 week before they even came round for the inspection visits.

Don't you just love banks?

Banks are still lending money for these projects but they have made it harder now and need more security from the client, shopping around is the answer and don't get put off by the first banks that say no. We went to 5 before we found one that would even think about loaning us the money.

Have a plan written down way before you go to these banks setting out what you need and just how you are going to repay them.

At the end of the day they are a business and just interested in what they can get out of you and how safe a risk you are so having it planed out will not only look better but increase your chances of them saying yes,

Always speak to the manager not the assistants. At the end of the day it is he who has the power or the contacts to get power to say yes and if you build up a relation with him or her that will help your chances.

Personally we did a reki trip first just going to a few and asking the assistant what sort of requirements they had about lending money for that sort of project then making appointment to see the manager armed with this info and your plans gives you a head start.

We did open 4 different accounts about 8 year before we thought about moving as this sometimes helps if you are not just a new account holder. I have had several different accounts here and always changed every few years.

Chapter 6

Papers needed for the house build

Anyone who knows me and who has followed me on my sites, knows just how much I hate paperwork and especially here in Spain where there seems to be just so much unnecessary paperwork for almost everything you want to do.

As Llani my Spanish wife had worked most of her life for local government office in Almeria city, she had some idea of what we needed and who we needed to see.

Also the architect we contracted Jose, run us through the proses and told us what order we needed to apply for the licences and permissions.

The architect will also tell you the correct order and where you need to present all these papers.

Llani having worked in government offices here was a godsend when it came to the paperwork and even she had times when it was far from straight forward so if your Spanish is less than perfect I would say pay to get help here it will be less painful.

Plans where first, I had been 1 year designing the house on a programme called Sketch up. All on my home pc. This program has loads of online YouTube training and is free to download but I later paid for a slightly better upgrade. There were others that I used that I list later on in the links page.

I also found some rough ground behind where I then lived and set it out on the floor in real scale to see just how much room I had in the bedrooms and corridors. Marking on the floor the beds and furniture really helps get a prospective of things and how they will look.

This I also did on the beach in the sand many times as it's easy to rub out and change.

My design was 4 bedrooms 2 bathrooms, one on suit and a large underground workshops and garage with gym area. 9m pool and swim up pool bar at the end.

You can see all these plans on my blog, links later on in the book.

I showed this to Jose and he said that it looked interesting and he had a few ideas of his own. We let him have a few days to show us. Later that week we returned and he showed us first what he had drawn up. It was just a basic design but really nothing like what we wanted way too cold and modern looking. All very square, not nice to look at.

We thought that we may fall out with him there and then but he just pushed it all to one side and said he would do whatever we wanted. Great and we got down to talking about my designs.

The only real thing I was not happy about with my design was the top floor layout. The rooms were all ok but the house did still look very square from the street.

He suggested that we turned the top floor about 45% to the right and this would change the look of the house and give us a better sea view from our main bedroom. We loved that idea and he suggested that the top floor corners could be round rather than 90%. Again we liked that idea but I was later to find the corners a lot of work fitted both with exterior brickwork and interior plasterboard.

Before we bought the land we did check just what we were allowed to build on that plot as some areas like ours do now have very strict rules on just what and how you can build.

Several years ago I did hear of a British couple who bought a plot of land very fast in the hills not far from me here in Almeria. They bought from estate agents who told them they had rights to build what they liked.

This they later found to be wrong and as the land was not as big as the agent had told them it was not until they presented the planes at the town hall that they found out they could not even build a house there, only farm buildings.

They went ahead anyway as the agent told them it would be ok just pay a small fine. Again this was wrong and after they finished the smaller than planned house that they and their 2 young boys would live in, they were not granted the first occupation licence or allowed to connect electric and water to the new finished house.

They ended up getting all gas appliances and have water delivered to a large underground tank they installed at great cost. They also paid a lot for some solar kits and this was all costing more and creating stress.

Finally after 2 years in the house they were ordered to get out by the local authorities and this created enormous stress for the owner who I knew and he had a mental breakdown.

Within 1 month they had sold the property for almost nothing and lost everything they had and returned to the north of England to move in with friends.

All this could have been avoided if they had done a few very basic checks first and not taken an estate agents word for it.

So once you have your land you need to apply for building permission and your architect will help with this and get your papers ready for presenting to the planning office and that's where the fun starts.

We presented 3 very large folders packed with very detailed plans on the build in great detail that had taken our architect 2 months to prepare. With these folders we went to the town hall planning office and had to fill in 5 different forms again in detail to present along with these folders and plans, Then just as we presented these folders and all the papers the lady told us we had to fill in one more paper, The paper was to tell them what all these papers were for. Crazy or what but the Spanish love their paper work and they hate trees...lol

Then you have to go to the bank and pay in full the tax on the build even before you have permission to start and that was 11.500k yes that is eleven and a half thousand euros just for the permission to start. It is refundable if turned down and it's a percentage on the cost of the build project.

Then once paid at the bank, you go back and show that you have paid and they take the folders to be reviewed,

It takes around 6 months.

We waited 7 months and went to the offices to ask how it was going and that was a big mistake.

We went in and asked to see who was in charge of our case and directed to a small office at the end of a long corridor. There was a young girl about 30 who was just on her way out and we asked her about our case. She was angry that we were there and said that she will get round to it and in her words **"it's ready when I say it's ready"** and she walked away.

How can you talk to people like that?

For me I like to distance myself from nasty negative people but sometimes you just can't get away from them

Later after telling our architect he said that most people don't go there as they don't know where to go and although its public offices and we have a right to ask she was upset about it and now our folders may get put at the bottom of the pile.

I asked a guy I knew who works in the town hall and he told me that this girl's dad is head of that department and she was a bit of a cow. We did get the plans passed but they had some things changed like no arches allowed, they had to be square and the front railings can't be painted black, they can be dark grey and the outside of the house had to be white. Why or what reason for these changes who knows but we can live with it.

It was 3 months longer though so I would say don't do what I did, just wait.

Within all these papers we presented are detailed health and safety papers and they have papers that you need to keep on sight that can be filled in or reviewed by an inspection visit, We did have just one inspection visit and they did ask for these papers and check all the workers working that day on out land.

Really the planning permission is the main papers to get started but there are papers like the water and electric papers that you apply for later on in the build. The town hall also has to come and give you a paper of the GPS of the property that's called the catastro. This basically says the plot and house is where it says it is on that land.

They are always a few feet out so don't worry, ours showed the front wall should have been 1 meter into the street but that was obviously impossible and they revised their details.

Then there are the noise pollution and insulation papers.

We had a guy come up when the house was almost finished and they put a big sound speaker outside the bedroom window and a mic inside and put on very loud noise and recorded the sound from inside, this gives a reading and a score that you have to register with the town hall.

When I went to buy the insulation I was told of a new geo thermic insolation that was the best and we went with that even though it was double the cost of what I was originally going to use. Worth doing though as later on when the house was built we did have a neighbour who's house is about 40m away have a party in the garden and with our windows shut we could not hear a thing.

Also this may be down to the fact that we put in very good double glazing. We had 18mm of glass, the outside pain was 6mm and 6 mm security glass then the thermal break of 18mm and another 6mm glass inside pain, So a total of 18mm of glass in all windows and doors.

No perseanas fitted "outside blinds" as I have had trouble with them in the past and the top boxes are never that well insulated. Not having them has really helped to the insulation and sound. We have curtains inside with nets.

Farther down the build line you will need these papers for water and electric.

Water licenses

When you are ready to have the water connected you need the local water company to come check that you have installed a water box in the wall and tapes for them to connect to. There is also a waste water connection paper you need, that is to take away your rain water and toilet water.

These are very strict conditions and I had a bid a headache with this and it took 3 months. Details and how we got over it in the problems chapter.

Electric license

Same here with the electric connections but this was easier not much but a little. Your electrician deals with most of this.

Both the water and electric is much faster to get sorted, just days if you are the promotor or months if you are not the promoter because it's in the name of the home owner so if that is you and you are the promotor, is way faster.

Bank papers

So many bank papers to fill in and get approved that can take weeks and most were related to our mortgage that was a little different as it was to build a new house and all tied in with the loan for the land. We wanted to get a mortgage for the whole thing land and house but that was not how the bank wanted it so we used our savings for the land and then had the banks money for the house build.

Once the house is finished in the eyes of the bank, you need to change it all as its now a house and not a house build, all a bit stressful and tricky to navigate and banks have different ways of doing it as we found out from our neighbours later on in our build as we got to know them better.

You need a final bank license to present to the town hall and this is from the bank that sends up a representative to walk around the house and see if everything is finished off.

 The painting and decorating is not that important, more like all the doors and windows fitted and all walls up, floors and roofs done things like that. You also have to pay the bank to come and do this and give you the papers that take about 2 weeks after they have been up but you still have to pay them weeks before they even come.

We had a mortgage from the bank and were told when we arranged it by the bank manager that we would have the money put in our account once we had the permission to build but this is not true. They had to send a person round every time we wanted money to see what we had spent the money on and we had to pay the bank. Or rather they took the money out of our bank. 250 euros each time we requested money and that was 5 times. Yes you have to pay them money to give you your own money. Welcome to Spain.

We requested about 15k each time until the last time when they give you the balance of your mortgage.

This was a real problem as we had to have certain things done before asking them to come and look, like all windows fitted all walls up all floors done things like that but remember you need to pay for all these materials and do the job before you get the money. This was a struggle at times for me and a few times my wife and I worked all weekends into the night to meet the requirements. If you pay trades to do your build you will need to pay them and all their materials way before you have the money from your bank.

This photo shows me moving around some dirt with one of my new toys.

I did love using this machine as it was great fun and very powerful. The arm on it extended to about 8m and had attachments that turned it into a Crain so very useful.

First occupancy papers

Once you want to live in the house you present the town hall with all these papers and licences so as they can give you the first occupation certificate that means you can now live in the house .I think I remember right that this comes before you can have the water and electric connected.

As we were 10 mins drive from the airport we also had to have papers from the airport to say all was ok. Things like our chimney that we had just 500mm higher had to get permission for that and yes more papers.

If you are having a Crain to help with the build then you will need permissions for that as well and that can cost thousands so check first, we went without and used high ab machine that had a crane hook that we use to load pallets to the roof. And lift stuff or would get the delivery drivers to use their Crain to life stuff up if needed.

Even though we were told what papers we needed it always seem there was just one more paper and that's just how it is here in Spain. Papers, papers and then more papers, on at least two occasions we had to fill in forms to say what all the papers were for when presenting them.

When you do present these papers make your own notes and dates of when you did what as this will come in handy later on. One great tip here is to ask that person's name and note it down. That makes them think why you are doing that and they just may be more careful with these papers that you have presented and you will always have a name if you need to go back and ask for help with the papers you have presented. Things will need to be redone or changes from time to time so creating good relations can't hurt.

Going into these places as often as we did means that they do get to know you so being friendly really makes sense.

Chapter 7

Laying the first bricks

It's always exciting to be able to lay the first brick and even before we had the correct permissions to start, I just couldn't wait any longer and was so excited to get started digging out the ground that was going to be the footings for the back wall.

This back wall was situated at the back end of the plot and would be the back garden wall running 20m long and 2m high with .5m below the ground.

My idea was to do it by hand with just a shovel as I didn't want to use a big digger machine as that would draw attention. By doing it by hand was really just a bit of fun and using my time as we waited for the permissions to come through.

This first wall was the back wall of the property and was cement blocks filled with cement to make them stronger as we get a lot of wind in this area. Also I fitted 6mm rebar on every 3 courses high to add strength and later cement plastered both faces and then the inside face was white Capa Fina plaster.

Below is the underground garage being shuttered up and concreate pour for the walls. It will be 3m underground and the house on top. That was around 1 month into the structure build that took 3 months in total.

As soon as the walls were up I was already working on waterproofing them from the outside as you will see later on.

The other photo shows that the concrete structure holds up the house so the walls are not load bearing at all and that means that if you place the piles in the right place you can have it as open as you like.

Some of the piles I build into the walls like in the lounge and bedrooms so as you don't notice them.

Flags up to show the top floor is done, well the floors anyway still have all the bricks to lay now.

Front view ground and first floors from the main street.

Only a few days later the guys started digging out the ground with big machines and diggers ready for the concreate pour. There was all of a sudden loads of people and work going on all over the plot so I could only get on with my wall to suit working around these guys, they had priority.

In the afternoons around 4pm when Llani got back from work, normally she finished at 3pm, she would help me mix cement and pass me the blocks that really were heavy and although at first a struggle for her, she soon started to get very strong.

There really was so much to do that I could not wait to get started even if my work was constantly interrupted by questions from the workers or just that I had to get out of the way. These blocks were the first blocks that we laid and it was the height of the summer so really hard going midday.

After 3 months when the structure of the house was up the first place I started laying bricks was in what was going to be the bathroom of the ground floor as we needed a place to shower and use a proper loo.

My plumber friend fitted us up an old second hand water heater that we connected to several extension leads and that gave us hot water and later a basic shower. The shower worked but the waste water went down into the garage into a large bucket as the plumbing was not yet connected and we had to empty this after each use.

There is a procedure to building a new house I know but we did things a little different as our needs were different as we were living on site.

In total we ended up laying 12500 blocks and bricks on the house build walls and then another 5000 on garden walls and flower boarders. All just Llani and I and all carried positioned and laid by us with all the cement mixed by small mixer mostly by Llani.

The hardest work of the build was the walls up on the top roof terraces as the terraces had walls of 1m high all around both terraces, each one being around 80sm.The reason these were hard is because all materials and cement had to come up 2 floors by small electric winch that I had bought and later once the walls were up we had to use the space where the chimney was going to be. Luckily our fire place was large 1m deep and 1m wide and 1 m high.

That meant that the chimney space was also large enough to pull up a small pallet loaded with bricks and buckets of cement. Later this was the main way of getting all materials up to the terraces and when it came to putting up the large flue pipe that was 300mm in diameter, I personally had to put on my rock climbing harness and shoes and pull it up along with myself, including any tools that where needed to do that job.

The sand we were getting delivered by the lorry load, much cheaper that way and that too had to mostly come up through the chimney space in large buckets .All the floors had 50mm of concreate on top of 50mm of insulation and again all up the same way or sometimes pulled up by hand with rope.

That's the pool dig out above 9m x 4m and 2m deep at the deep end.it was spray on concreate from a machine at high pressure with

fibre in it to add to the strength. All walls and floors had a lot of rebar as well.

Looking back a Crain would have been time saving but we did save again here by not having one. One other point here about the Crain is that my neighbours had one put on his plot for his build and after they took it down there was this large reinforced concreate slab that was about 3m square and 1 meter thick left in his garden that later meant that the deep end of his pool could only be 1.5 deep because of the position of this slab.

Worth noting if you are going to have a Crain that you get its position right first time and better to make the base for it deeper than you need as you can cover it over after.

For me the brick laying part was enjoyable as Llani and I, plus occasionally Marta, Llanis daughter, would have the music on and the sun was out and life was great because we were building our dream home.

Looking back now at the finished house Llani and I often think how did we do all that work. At 59 now the both of us just could not do it again and wished we could have done it much earlier in life but that's what everyone would say I am sure.

The time was right for us then and we almost didn't do it.

Many nights we would get into bed after an exhausting day bricklaying and feel all the aches and pains but fell asleep really fast.

Days flew by the first few months and it took us around 2 months to get all the exterior walls up.

We did have it all done ready to live in within 2 years but there will be a few years yet before we can say it's really finished and probably it never will as I feel it's a job for life and to be honest I don't mind doing it till I drop.

When I think of people saying that they can't wait till they retire I think if you love what you are doing then you don't want to retire ever. It's just a case of finding something that you love doing that pays the bills.

Chapter 8

Best price for materials

When it comes to materials I really feel I have a talent for getting the best prices from builder's merchants and almost any store here in Spain. There are a few tricks I use that seem to work well time after time and here I will share these with you and give you links to places all over Spain where you can get the best prices.

One thing I will point out here is that if you put your name down on the house build when you start as the promotor then you don't pay 21% tax its just 10% tax and that can save you thousands on materials and costs.

It costs nothing to do this but you need to make sure you have insurance as you are then the person responsible for the build including health and safety but it was no big deal and did save us thousands. Also later on this is an advantage when it comes to getting water and light connected as if you are the promoter and the owner it gets down faster.

For my new house build I used one main supplier for most of my materials that has been amazing and is available all over Spain.

Leroy Merlin.

They have branches all over Spain and are like the UK equivalent of B and Q.

Now there are some things that are just better off getting at main builders suppliers like sand and cement and bigger materials like concrete beams and metal materials like rebar and steel.

The first thing you need to do is get a PRO card. Most people know about their green card where you get discount or points back for the money you send but the pro card is way more and still free just ask in store near you.

The pro card or V.I.P card as they sometimes call it, works the same way but with better discounts and more points and money off, PLUSS you get deliveries cheaper and a personal assistant that you can call anytime day or night to prepare your order so as its ready and waiting to pick up when you arrive. Also the store is open to these Pro card holders from 7am till way after the store is closed to the public and this means many times I have been the only one in the store.

They have a goods entrance that you can use to enter with a pro assistant to take you through the store so as you don't need to que up at cash tills, it's done by them in the back and they often have private parking for pro card holders.

You also get things like T shirts clothing and other free bees and invited to special promotions and BBQ in the summer with all food and drink.

I also negotiated a great deal for my deliveries way cheaper than most pro card holders get and all because I told them I was building my new house and would be buying a lot from them.

Many times I just needed a few things so ordered them on their website from home and they put them on their next delivery that was going near my house so I only paid the minimum for that delivery and sometimes free.

If I ever saw a product the same cheaper in another store anywhere not just their stores, they would match it so with the points system it turned out even cheaper.

With the personal assistant you can call them and they get you help from their top experts on any question you may have. Remember many of their staff are sent on training courses for the products that they sell so as they can answer all these questions. That means with just a phone call to your assistant, you can get all the latest info and help on any project you are doing and what's the best or cheapest way to do it.

I was invited to go to their staff room on a promotion for paint and while there saw a name board with all the pro card holders in that area. I asked what that was and was told that all staff are trained to look at that board and remember your name and face as they have a photo of you when you get the card. I am always greeted with a hi from staff some of whom I have never seen before but they still say hi and use my name.

During the Covid business we were not allowed out for months here and that I thought would be the end of our building here but no.

I just called them up and ordered over the phone what I needed or from the website and it was delivered that day or the next, right to my door so we could continue working even when nobody else was.

They also had masks and clothing that we bought at this time as we could not get out.

For things like sand and bigger items that Leroy's did not have or could not match the prices, I went to 2 of my local builder's merchant's and told them that I was building a new house and what was the best price they could do if I bought most of my materials there. Often they gave me little better rates on sand and cement bricks and blocks and then I would take these prices to Leroy Merlin to see if they could match it.

This was a game but worth doing as I was getting cement and sand for really silly prices and as I had a trailer they gave me even better prices as they would fill my trailer up at the builder's merchants loose, no bags.

I did the same with steel and beams in 2 other builders' stores and got great prices in both. A few I tried that were smaller or not run by a boss but franchises could not do me discounts.

Wood was the same, I found a few timber yards and again told them I was going to buy loads even if I was not they still gave me some discounts and the ones that I visited frequently gave me very good service. In the sand and cement places many of them they would load me up with bags that were slightly split or damaged that where fine but just could not sell to public as they were damaged.

On one run I was asked if I wanted 5 pallets of bricks that were small boarder bricks. All for free so as they could make room in the stores yard, so I just paid delivery for the bricks, all 5 pallets of them that I used to build my flower boarders in my garden, all free.

You will need to buy new tools as well when building a house even though I had most things I needed working here for years as a builder here, I still needed some specialized tools and new tools.

Find a good tool shop and again see what deals they do. One store I needed a power saw, cement mixer and scaffold tower and got a cordless drill included for free.

Building a new house you will often need a lot of something like screws and nails so these people will do deals with you when you buy a lot of something. One store I needed nails for my nail gun and they showed me a box of 500, I ask what if I bought 1000 of each size. Then the price comes right down. Always worth a try and one tip that really works is I always try and be really friendly and place my hand on the guys shoulder and say, " come on what's the best price you can help me with" always use the word help as people like to help if they can.

Remember keep factoras "receipts" for everything as once after a few months a grinder I bought stopped working as I was really pushing it hard, they got it repaired for free saving me money.

When you go to these stores try and find out where they get these materials from. One timber yard I use to go to for years I did this and found that they got the wood straight off the boat in Almeria and had a yard there. I went to that yard that was not really open to the public and was able to buy some larger stuff there and way cheaper prices.

They would not cut anything as it was all around 6meters long but I always took along my portable generator and power saw to cut it to the right length there and put it on my trailer that was ok with stuff up to 4m long.

Buying timber sawn not planed is way cheaper and my planer cost 300 euros but saved me that on timer costs. Yes it's a bit more work running it through the planner but I feel worth it.

Personally I found it best to buy timber long as it seemed to be the most economical way to go and we did use a lot of timber considering that the house was brick and concreate.

Tiles are not expensive in Spain as most are made here and there are so many great tile and marble places all over Spain but we went with mostly porcelain ass that is way harder and harder wearing and looks great. The price for porcelain here is pretty good and we went to a large store here in Almeria and agreed with them a great deal if we bought all porcelain for the house from them. We also used their tiles for walk ways in the patios and garden and got best prices as I picked most of it up in trips with my trailer. Also with porcelain some of the tiles that we used in the bathroom and kitchen were 2m long and so have way less joints and just look amazing.

It all has a high gloss finish and reflects the light so makes the house very bright all day.

Below is the unfinished hall way and stairs that I did in all porcelain and the floor tiles are 75mm square so really big and we love them. The hand rails I still need to do but will be iron railings with wooden hand rails.

You can also see my idea of the wooden panelling on the walls that we followed in all the halls and up the stairs.

Shipping container was well worth having not just for the tools and material but as a place to sit out of the August sun and of course make the tea.

We did buy special door locks for it off Amazon as there was a lot of tools and materials in it over night when we were not there.

The trailer I had was often backed up against the doors with locks and chains on that as well. It never can be too much in my view.

Chapter 9

Squatting in my own garage

Yes we really did this for several months even in the winter with no walls.

So the plot of land was in Almeria near the airport and we were staying at that time in my wife's house that she had been left to her by her decease parents. Half was hers and half was her sisters who now lived in Granada.

It was a pretty old house in a very small village in the hills of Fiñana, about 1 hour drive from our new plot of land and house build, on the Granada road.

Once we sold our apartment we had to move up there with what we had and so every time we wanted to visit the plot of land it was 1 hour each way. Not ideal so we did look into buying a caravan but that would be difficult to place in the right spot on the land and needed permissions. Also we looked into renting nearby but now we were moving to a nicer area it was also much more expensive to rent there. Rather glade we didn't go with the caravan though because some time later I knew a couple who were building a new house that same time as us and they bought one for 8k and said it was a mistake as it was very cold at nights unless they had the heating on all night and daytimes it was like a sauna.

Here am I me plastering the garage corner we will use as a temp bedroom.

One job I liked doing but it really is the messiest job in the world and it goes everywhere no matter how well you try and be careful.

All this rent money would eat into out materials budget so decided the drive was not great but more economical to do.

The structure was really just the garage floor and walls with the piles that held up each floor, no walls any were except the garage that had these half-finished concrete walls and open small window with large open garage wall were the garage door would one day be.

I made some temporary steel sliding doors to use the garage as a lock up and we had a container I was renting on the land that was full of builder's materials and tools. Once the construction of the garage and the piles was finished we could start on bricking up the walls but the acro supports were still needed to be in place for 3 more weeks so it was fun walking around a house with all these hundreds of acros holding up floors and ceilings, no real room to move.

As the garage was the first place we pored the cement it was the first place dry enough to take down the acros and after 3 weeks we did and that opened up the underground garage.

I suggested to my wife that these trips 1 hour home and back were losing me time if I was to work here and that if I stayed in the garage I could start early and finish late and not have to drive 2 hours every day.

Llani was working just 18 mins from our new house build so it was better for her as well and after we worked on the house a few weeks we knew that we needed to move into the garage,

At the back corner of the garage where my workshop was going to be, I put up a wall and made a 3m square room with just certain to close it off.

I plastered the walls and ceiling in that area alone and that was our bedroom for 12 months.

We had a porta loo on sight and for the first 12 months that's all we had, even in the middle of the night if you needed a pee you had to go up through all the scaffolding with a torch and across the muddy plot to the porta loo that had no lights.

After a week I made a portable shower in the corner of the garage with a shower curtain and sink and the waste was just a bucket. No hot water we didn't have that for 3 months.

Each night when we went to bed we had to barricade the doors up with wood and iron bars and use an extension lead to the street electric supply for power. The very first few weeks we didn't have power so had to use a small generator I bought but that could only be use 1 hour at a time and not all night.

Solar and battery packs were our life line for months and it was real basic camping on a very low level but good fun and we did have a laugh at times.

One night we invited 2 of our best friends to come have dinner at our new house. They sat with us in the garage at a wooden table I had knocked up and we had takeaway pizza and beer all sitting on buckets as chairs.

It was hard going at times but cold showers were not that bad really till November and because we got up early and went to bed late we got so much more done.

Most of our friends were shocked at how we were living and thought we couldn't do it for long but we really did get used to it and in time moved up to the first bedroom I made on the ground floor and started to use the bathroom on the ground floor that was the first thing I started on.

Later we moved into the second bedroom that was a bit bigger and then finally up again to the top floor and into our own bedroom and on suit. It was real luxury each time we moved. Looking back now we often think how did we live like that but at that time we were so involved in the house build that sleeping arrangements were not that important and the need to save money on renting some apartment or house drove us to camping out in the garage.

Each week living in the garage I did make improvements like a work top and camping gas to cook on then take away the bucket shower I made and replace it with a camping shower head, that was luxury for a while especially when we had hot water fitted.

Chapter 10

Be your own project manager

A project manager is a person who has some knowledge of building that is in overall charge of the build and sees that all goes ok and answers onsite questions or gets you answers from the related trade's people.

Many people pay top money as a good project manager will save you time and money and really help the build go smoothly.

On this build it was going to be me, as I had been in the building industry many years and worked as a project manager on smaller jobs in both the UK and in Spain but being maintenance manager on Brighton Pier for several years was a real eye opener as to getting things done and working in crazy weather conditions with multiple trades all working in very tight and dangerous work places.

Right from the first week I saved myself several hundred euros as we needed more gravel on the ground dig out than was calculated but after some research by me I found that we could still stay within the permitted requirement's with 6 lorry loads less and that it would make no difference to the base as we were already increasing the steel amount and hardness of the concreate as it was classed a earthquake risk area.

Then there was the rubbish clearance that needed to be certificated at a registered depot. We were going to be digging out 200smeters of dirt 4m deep just for the underground garage and that all had to be taken away and then later bought back to fill in.

I spent many hours trying to calculate these amounts as I didn't want to pay to bring in dirt for the back fill when we had so much of it here already.

There was a plot behind ours that they had not yet started on and I arranged with them to let us store it there for a few months but that soon reached 3m high and we needed more room.

Some had to go and this would cost around 200 a lorry to get rid of it. In all about 10 lorry's full, so expensive and this money could buy us more materials.

I had an idea when I was driving home one afternoon about the golf course that was just behind us. So I went and asked to see the manager and asked if they needed any dirt, as we were building and it was good clean dirt that may be useful for the golf course.

All I wanted was him to sign a receipt saying that we had given it to them for free so as I could use that when I needed to show where we dumped to rubbish.

He liked that idea and I had the next 10 lorry's take it to the back of the course where he wanted to store it.

Being project manager I was always looking out for possible dangers and problems and moved cables and pieces of wood or rebar out of the way of the workers, this I am sure stopped several accidents from occurring.

One day as everyone was in full swing all working hard, a few guys up on the top floor preparing the rebar for the next concrete pour and a few below cutting the wood supports, all power went dead, everything just stopped.

Looking at me they shouted. "No power "and I had to drop everything I was doing to go investigate. One of the power leads to the temporary electric supply had pulled out and was broken. Not repairable so we needed a new one fast. This particular one was the main one that everything runs off and the plug was different and of course we didn't have one on site.

I jumped on my motorbike and set off for the hardware store that was only about 10 mins away but everything sort of came to a stop as they all needed power for what they were doing at that time. On my trip to the store I was thinking about all those guys waiting for me and that we had a cement lorry coming in about 1 hour so I had to get one and fast.

Luckily the store did have one and that problem only took about 45 mins to sort out. These are the little things that can cost a lot of money, like if the cement lorry turned up early and we had no power we could not pour as there was no liberator to help settle the concrete and that wet concrete waits for nobody.

Most days I would try and think of all the possible things we would need that day and what could go wrong and how we could get over it fast but it's almost impossible to think of everything and there is always that little thing that will happen when you least expect it.

A project manager has this experience and can keep these problems from escalating so is worth his money if you find a good one.

These are just a few of the ways I made things run smoothly and there were many other problems I detail in the problems chapter that a good project manager will find solutions for .

Some friends of my wife's are now about to start a smaller new house build not far from us and they said that his wife will be doing what I did.

I wish them well but she will also be working full time as a nurse here at the local hospital so I really can't see how she can do it and I am sure she will create more stress and holdups for their build if they don't get someone in to be project manage.

This was one reason a good friend of mine ended up losing everything here as I described earlier in the book, he had no real idea and took it all on himself and that just became too much in the end and the stress really made him ill.

There's going for it and taking risks and just being strong but there is a point when you need to know your abilities and just pay someone to help. A project manager just a few days a week would be better than none at all and your architect will have some he can recommend.

Remember there will always be people dropping by the site once its started and the workers there are busy in what they are doing so things can go missing and you don't know who's walking about the place if nobody is watching out for them.

One of my neighbours did pay a young lad to sleep in a hut on the plot just to keep an eye out but I think he was asleep most of the times II drove by.

Chapter 11

Enjoying the unfinished house

Being on site all day every day, it was important for us to have moments of relaxation or at least enjoy the house, even though it was far from finished and we did this many times.

The guys we had doing the structure were only here for a short time really but each lunch time I would sit down with them and have a chat and as it was the summer months they would made a small fire and do a BBQ or even a few times a full paella.

Once they had left, Llani and I would often gather up some rubbish in the way of wood and do our own BBQ over some bits of steel rebar that were everywhere.

No grass down or tiles finished but we still used the pool.

On one such occasion we had a lovely layout of sardines and without notice our architect turned up for a quick visit so had a few sardines off our BBQ.

In the evenings when we were all alone we would go to the top floor on the roof and just sit there with a glass of wine or beer looking at what we had done that day and visualizing how it will turn out.

As soon as the top floor was done the tradition is to hoist up the Spanish flag. So the builders put up this flag they had that was about 2m long and I bought the union Jack to go along side it. It did get the neighbours attention.

At the end of the summer not all the walls were up yet and Llanis aunt said she and her husband were coming down from Madrid to stay with us.

Here am I out on the bike having a breather and just enjoying the sun and warm air.

The bike I had bought several years back and that was my second one like that and was very handy in running to get small stuff although I have collected a bag of sand of cement on the back of it when needed.

I really think they thought that after seven months we had finished the house but after a chat Llani told them how it was going but they still insisted they were coming for 3 days. We arranged a hotel that's just 5 mins drive from us and they stayed there but every day they were at the house build trying to help out.

One afternoon when Llani finished work she came home to see her aunt mopping the lunch floor with a mop and bucket even though there were no walls and just a rough cement floor full of dust. The Spanish are obsessed with cleaning here.

Lunch times I would gather some blocks and build a make shift table from the blocks and wooden boards and we had lunch sitting on old chairs that the builders had left behind that were broken.

As there were still no new walls in the lounge area just open views, the birds would fly in and eat the bits off the floor and often we would have them land on the table right where we were eating and as time went on they became very unafraid of us.

After living in the garage for several months we moved to the ground floor once the bathroom was finished there and then into the next bedroom as that was bigger and then finally the top floor our own on suit.

The pool was not on our list as it was expensive and we had planned to put one in later once the house was completed.

Then after really thinking about how much trouble that may be, we decided that we should do it now. So we contracted a guy and his mate to dig out the pool area.

It was again my design that I also did on Sketch up and it was 9m long 4 m wide and 2 meters deep at the deep end and 1m at the shallow end.

This was a bit different though as I had designed a swim up bar at one end.

That meant that there would be a slope at the deep end on one side so as people could walk up to the seating bar at the end of the deep end that was just below the water line, like a long seat that faces the end of the pool looking out.

Later I would build a full size bar at the end of the pool with a serving hatch so as we could pass drinks to people sitting it the pool at the seating end.

The first year we just painted the walls of the pool white and filled it up with water so as we could use it and it was amazing to be able to have a swim in our own pool whenever we wanted.

The second year we finally agreed on the tiles we wanted and Llani and I spent 2 weeks tiling it and then this last summer we started enjoying it again.

Even before the house was finished and before we had any cement around the pool we were swimming in it and enjoying it.

This last year we bought a volley ball net and strung that across the pool and have had so much fun with our friends.

Then I bought a swim cord off Amazon that's just a belt with an elastic cord that you fix at one end of the pool and can swim all day and not go anywhere. That was a real bargain and now I have designed and made an even better one that works much better.

My underground workshops will be the last thing that gets finished but I am always down there pottering about making or working on something and I love it there.

Several times our friends have invited us to there's for dinner or lunch and we have gone a few times but both of us feel very guilty after for not working on the house.

At the back end of the house I have an allotment area that's 4m wide by 15 meters long and walled off from view. This is just a hobby for me and something I thought would keep be occupied later in life but I find myself drawn there each day and have planted some seeds that have already given us peppers tomatoes and radishes. The melons are doing nicely now and so are several other vegetables.

My plan is to try and grow as much fruit and veg as we can that we normally buy and also some fruit trees. Later I want to have a budgie aviary there as well but that's a sore point with the wife at the moment.

At the end of the garden near the pool I made a seat bench with an arch in wooden trellis that goes overhead one side to the other and we planted a passion flower at each end and that has now met in the middle and has amazing flowers on it, so nice to sit under at the end of the day and just look back at the house to see how it's coming on.

We have had several pool parties even though the house is not finished and once the pool bar is up and running next summer we will be having an amazing house warming party and anyone who buys any of my books and gives them a nice review on Amazon will be automatically added to the party list for nest summer.

One of my wife's cousins has all the equipment for local fiestas and so he will be helping us set it all up so should be fun.

Chapter 12

Going Green energy

When first designing the house I was very keen to go green with solar energy as much as possible, not just to keep the bills down but to do our bit for the environment but this later turned out to be very difficult and expensive.

Originally I wanted all solar power and go off grid but after speaking to 3 different company's they told me that I would need 16 large solar panels that would cover all of one of my roof terraces and some of the second terrace, Then there are the large batteries needed that would be in a separate lockup in the garage taking up room.

Even then we would need to be connected to the main grid as they told me there may be days in winter when we needed to take energy from the grid. The days of selling it back to the electric companies is over, or if you can arrange it they pay next to nothing for it.

The cost of those systems were all pretty much the same and came in at around 20k. The cheapest quote I had being 19k and the most expensive being 28 k. Now that can pay my electric bills here for most of the rest of my life, so why would we do it? Going green is a great idea but still not practical here yet which I find ridiculous as Spain gets so many sunny days all year round.

We did have 2 solar panels and a 300 ltr tank on the top roof terrace to heat the how water for the house and that is working out great.

In the garden both my neighbours have extensive garden lighting all from the mains and have complained at their electric bills, so we have all solar lights in the garden that are very good coming on every night when the sun goes down and costing nothing to run. We have mains lighting in the garden if needed but only 2 lights that we never need to have on. Once the garden is completed and full of trees and plants I will fit many more solar lights to create more atmosphere.

Later on my plans are to fit some sort of wind turbine to generate electric but how big and where I will put it is still under review. Going green is the right thing to do I know that but costs are what is stopping most doing more, especially when it comes to solar.

Solar in Spain has come down in price over the years especially since they changed the energy minister here a few years ago so now there is not as much tax on the sun as there use to be here. Yes the Spanish did tax the sun.

Above is the front door that I made the week we bought the land. I made it in our house in the hills while we were waiting for papers to come through and the house was designed around this. It was from teak hardwood that I handmade and jointed and all the iron work I also did except the ring knocker.

I found that in an old reclaim yard in Seville on a weekend break some years before and made a back plate for it. The side lamps I also made from large steel spoons bought from the local shop and the lamp on the ceiling was made by me as well. All lights have flickering bulbs so look like flames at light.

There is an unfinished Tudor rose that I am carving in the frame above the door that's taking me some time. All the roof beams are wood and I also made and fitted them, they are the castle influence bit that Llani likes from our Scotland trip.

Chapter 13

Problems and how we got over them.

In all we did pretty well and not that many problems really but there were a few things that cost us money, time and a lot of stress and here I will list them.

I normally don't like to dwell on problems just find solutions and try and forget the bad things just remember all the good but I feel its important to give a heads up on the problems we had and I know everyone will experience different problems these may help you avoid ours or give you an idea how to better handle yours.

First was the builders who we contracted to build the house gave us a set price for the structure but when it came to the footings for the front porch they told us that was not included and would be 2500 euros more, just for the footings as they needed so much reinforcing bar.

We were not happy with this and went through all our papers but found nothing to say it was or was not included and argued it for a few days.

In the end I suggested that they pay for it and I would do all the backfilling of dirt around the house if they let me use there digger machine.

They had contracted a guy to do the back filling and that was about the same amount so they agreed. I had never driven a machine that big and you need permission to drive it but as it was on my land I was the owner and the driver it was ok. So a quick lesson on the controls from them and I was off. Remember all this dirt I had place on the empty plot behind us and it was 3m high and covered most of that plot.

I worked 8 hours a day for 7 days and bought the fuel, hard work but it is done and one more problem erased.

Then the first guys who we contracted to do the white plaster of all the outside walls started and the very first day they turned up there was only 2 guys, even after the boss had said there would be 6. No machine lift that they said either.

That was on its way the boss told me.

Then I get a call from a local hire company that I have dealt with for a few years here and the boss said he had this guy in his shop saying that they wanted a lift machine and that it was to be put on my account in my name and I would pay for it at 600 a week rent for 2 weeks.

I was mad and we almost through them off there and then.

I also told the boss I wanted to see all the papers to make sure they were all registered to work. If not the new rules here means we the owners can be fined 10k for each worker without papers and responsible for the health cover for life if anyone has an accident.

The papers the boss told me would all be there the next day.

The next day the machine turned up that we agreed the boss would pay for as it was all included in the price, just the materials I would buy and they were already here on site waiting.

The machine was dropped off and after just 10 mins a pipe broke and oil pumped out all over the land about 20 litres of it.

Then I went to the hire shop and got the right machine for the job and found out that this boss guy wanted the cheapest old machine they had. I changed that and things started again after 3 days of sitting around.

Then at the end of the first week I paid the boss the money we agreed on and all seemed ok,

Next Monday morning and a few of the workers turned up and not happy saying that they had not been paid.

When asked they said their boss had told them I had not paid him.

We got him back that morning and I had it out with him. He said it was all ok and he would pay his guys at the end of the next week once I paid him.

This was all wrong and I told him it's over and to leave. After a bit of arguing he left and I pulled one guy aside who seemed like he knew what he was doing and told him I would pay him to help me do it all with him if he left his boss.

He jumped at it and that when I found out none of them were legal here all working for cash that the boss paid them when he felt like it.

So I contracted this guy on his own, I paid his self-employed payments for 3 months and insurance.

■■

I have loads of videos and blog posts on my sites about going self-employed and yes and that is how I got started here and feel it a great way for others. All details on my blog.

✳✳✳✳✳✳✳✳✳✳✳✳✳✳✳✳✳✳✳✳✳✳✳✳✳✳✳✳✳✳

Once you go self-employed here the first time, you can start off with paying 70 a month for the first year and then it goes up in stages till it reaches 300 a month.

It was long hard days but we got it done after about 3 months.

Artificial grass

We were expecting an inspecting from the council to see that the house was finished so needed to have the grass down.

We originally wanted tiles over most of the garden area but there was a rule where we were that a percentage of the land needed to be green area and that meant artificial grass or dirt with flowers.

We went for the artificial grass but that took us a time researching.

First off there are so many different types you can have and now even colours. Red, blue and black are now available. Costs to can range from 8 euros a sm to 48 euros a sm. At our build we needed 200sm so could be very expensive.

We called several places to get free samples sent that all came very fast but they all looked very similar but with very different price tags.

Our neighbour had fitted some on his garden so we went and had a look, he had paid around 25 euros a sm but it did look great.

Then several weeks later the guys next door fitted theirs and that was different again and just added more confusion into the pot for us. Finally we thought we would go with the same as the guys next door who had paid around 15 euros for 38mm thick. Then there's the glue and fixing tape around another 500 euros and labour.

When we were ready to buy the grass we went to the same shop and they had run out and said they didn't know when they would have more in but there was another one nicer but much more expensive.

So back to getting more samples from other places and soon we almost had enough small square samples to do the entire garden.

Finally we found a main dealer in Albox that was 1 hour drive from us that had a great deal so took the trailer and went to see what they had.

They had just had a new delivery of the latest artificial grass in from Madrid and it was 40mm thick and much more compact with a 20 year guarantee. It was 20 euros a sm so with the glue and tape over 4000 euros about twice what we had originally budgeted for but was just so good we had to get it.

We found a guy locally that had fitted our neighbours grass so went with him at a cost of 500 for fitting but it was worth it as he did a great job and it's not as straight forward as I first thought it would be.

The grass is great and although we didn't really want it in the beginning, it is one of the best things we did at the house build and very comfortable around the pool plus looks amazing.

The jobsworth water man

We had an inspection to connect the water from the street to our house and this needed to be connected to a box and tap in the front wall of our house at street level.

Now my plumber had told me they we very strict and that it needed to be a 700mm high no less and right in front of where the street connection was.

He showed me just where the box in the wall needed to be fitted and what height I needed to put it and let me get on with it. The problem was that our front wall was not meant to be higher than 600mm with railings on top of that so after speaking to my architect he told me it would be ok to build the box into the wall to the right were there was a brick support post.

A few days later I had built this plastic box into the wall and had my plumber come put a tap in it all ready for the water company to connect it up.

Then the water man came and saw it. "NO, NO, NO," he said, "can't have that it's in the wrong place it needs to be right in front of the Street connection".

I explained that if I did that I would have to make the wall higher to take the box and the council rule was no higher than 600mm for the wall.

What about if I put in a bit lower at 500mm. No it has to be 700 high so I asked why and he said "it's so as the guy who comes and checks it does not have to bend down", even though the house in front and both my neighbours did this he was not having it. We didn't get on well and he left in a hurry.

So I had to take out that section of railings cut them all down and make the wall in that area higher, even though we may have problems with the council but we can't possible keep them both happy doing it how they both wanted so that was it, I moved it up and over. This took me all week to do.

Then we called this lovely gentleman back to inspect it again.

He turned up and said begrudgingly **"looks ok"** but then opened the street manhole cover where the water went down in front of our house and said "the pipes dirty".

I looked at him and said "yes that's dirty water going down there".

"You need to clean the pipe" he said I told him that's the council's pipe and not mine, but he insisted we needed to clean it so I told him to wait I get the hose. "No it has to be done right" he said and that means paying a company with a jet wash to do it and he wanted to see the receipt.

Again off he went and I was fuming. We paid a company 45 euros to wash the inside of their pipe and called this Mr Jobsworth back again.

He looked at everything in detail including the box and tap he had already inspected and then said "the top of the manhole cover was 2cm too far to the right".

At first I thought this was a joke and he was having me on but he was serious. Now out comes my wife as she has seen me getting heated.

He told her we need to get the lid moved over 2cm so as it sits correctly on the top even though it's not ours and the council fitted it. We still need to pay to get it put right. Off he went again and I was not a happy chappy I can tell you.

My architect told us that we were right here and that we could get the council to do it but that could take months for them to even come and look at it.

So we begrudgingly got it moved over by a company who dug up the cement and re fitted it and re bedded it in new cement and cleaned it all up. This cost another 50 euros and 5 days later down the road.

So back he comes again, Mr Jobsworth for another inspection.

Again he went over everything and even put his hand inside the pipe to see it was clean, I almost pushed him down the bloody pipe and shut the lid.

He gave the certificate to my wife and we could now call the water company to come connect our water. For this last connection we would need them to dig up the road and connect their pipe to ours and that cost 2800 euros, that's a fixed price that only the council can do.

That was probably the most stressful part of the whole build but all totally avoidable if we had got a rational, logical person rather than a power hungry Mr Jobsworth.

These inspectors do like the power they think they have and they do like to feel so important.

When we had the bank send a reprehensive round for the inspection to see that we had reached the next stage to release our mortgage money, they once sent a woman of about 40 in heels and a hard hat, all looking like she know what she was doing but she really had no idea and said that the internal brick walls looked nice so I had to tell her they were plaster board. She didn't want to go up onto the roof terrace to take the obligatory photos as she was frightened of heights, so I went up there with her camera and took photos for her and remember we had to pay the bank 250 for these inspections to release our money.

The last time they sent a guy he was in his late 60s and walked with a limp and seemed on deaths door as he could hardly walk. He looked around and took just 2 photos and I asked if that was enough and he responded we have loads of photos of this house now. What was the point god knows. And remember it's only to get them to give us our own money that they agreed in the mortgage. If ever we defaulted or spent the money of anything else they could always just take the house so would never lose out.

These visits really got to me as a real waste of time and my money.

The container

We rented a 6m long shipping container to use as a lock up for all the tools and materials on site and arranged for it to be delivered.

The day came and the driver turned up and asked where he was to place with his Crain.

After I showed him he set it down and said "Do you have a ladder",

When I asked him why he said "to get up on top and take off the chains that the Crain he had used to load it". "But that's your job" I told him

"No I have vertigo" he said and would not go up there, what your joking right? "No you have to do it" so I climbed up on top and disconnected his chains and off he went. For that I also paid 90 euros.

These are not that bad really but at the time they did cause me some stress and at times I wanted to pull my hair out but that's all part of the dream I guess and goes with the adventure of building a house in Spain.

Luckily we didn't have any real major problems but several hold ups and remember we started just as the covid restrictions started to come in so it could have been a lot worse if we had to have companies working here full time like most other builds.

Working on the house mostly on my own meant that I didn't really need to wait much for others but things did take time. That was not really a problem as I was working for free on my own house and the work never really seemed like work as it was all for us. Working on some client's projects at times I got fed up and some days just didn't want to be there but never did I feel that way working on my own house build, in fact the opposite I love every day of it all except the days with Mr Jobsworth from the water company.

Running a building business here many years I really loved the work here most days especially working in this amazing weather in Spain that beats the UK weather any day.

Most days working in a T shirt and shorts even in winter months just makes such a difference to life but idiots like this water guy do get you down but we still have guys like this in the Uk so I guess it better to deal with them here in the sun than there in the rain.

Chapter 14

Build Costs

Here's where I will list costs of as much as I can remember but there are more costs on my blog under David's dream house build.

Land 148k plus taxes that's another 25 k on top

Total land costs 173k

The structure build we contracted my architect's brothers company and that cost 97k this is paid in 3 stages.

Architects fees 16k again paid in 3 stages

Structural architects fee 3500 euros

Building and planning licensees 12k need to be paid in full upfront.

Electricians costs total 12k you agree payment plan

Plumbers costs 6k

Materials for total build so far around 120k

Pool cost 8000 euros

Water to fill it up was 320 euros. It was 50,000 litres.

Tiles for pool another 2000 euros, could have done this much cheaper but Llani has expensive taste I guess and we loved what we picked.

Other Labour cost around 5k as I did most of the work myself.

Rental of equipment 800 euros

The container we rented to store materials on site 1200 euro, I could have bought one for 900 but then you have to try and sell it.

I had to buy around 3000 euros of tools and the trailer I bought was new cost 1200 euros. This saved us a lot overall and still is very useful.

Connection charges for water and electric around 600 euros and the street connection for waste water was 2800 euros. You have to pay the council to do this and it's a fixed price.

Sound and insulation test was 300 euros. This just takes about 1 hour but still expensive but required here now.

Registry fees 400 euros

Notary fees around 200

There are possibly a few small costs as well but I have listed some of these in posts on my blog along with the videos and photos.

So total cost to date around 480,000 euros

The bank valued the house just before it was finished and no pool for 720,000

My neighbour has had his valued as have the people in front and all on the same size plot with same 4 bedrooms and pool; one was valued at 835,000 euros, the other at 900,000 euros.

We were told by an estate agent friend that he thought our house should be around 850,000 euros once totally finished.

You could ask an architect to give you costs of the build but it all depends on materials you use and the labour you use. You get what you pay for but it's a real juggling act.

Most of the trade's people working on my house earned around 120 a day. Electricians 150 and tilers were the most expensive at 200 a day so that's why I did almost all the tiling myself.

Chapter 15

Top tips to save time money and stress

Here in this chapter I will give my top tips that will save you money, time and stress and tell what I would do differently if I was to do it again. I would not, lol

A trip to your local planning registry office is a must even before you buy and property or land as they can tell you so much about that land or property like what permissions it has and just what you can or can't build on there.

It's all free to do this and if you're Spanish is basic then take a Spanish speaking friend or pay someone as it's really worth it and you will learn so much.

On one plot I was interested in buying we found out from the planning officer that there was a new water pipe deep under the land that belonged to the water company and that nothing was to be built in that corner of the property not even a wall as it was possible they needed to come dig it up one day. This was not told to us by the agent or owner when we looked at that plot and could have been a real problem for us so we pulled away from that one.

The planning registry officers also had the latest satellite images of every plot and property that are updated regularly and very informative about that property or land you may want to buy, so go see them and get all the info you can. Even if it's to see what's over the wall of your neighbours.

Some nice new tools are now on the job.

First off research is always the key and we did a lot of research and we were lucky that we knew a few people in the trade, so to speak, as I had been working in Spain in the building industry for some time. If you have found a property or plot then go speak to the neighbours in that area as they will tell you a lot about the people and the area. Ask them about that property or land, often they know things others don't. Most times it's just gossip but could provide you with new leads to follow or new information.

Drive around and see what places are like at night. If you see a plot or property you like then go there at different times of the day and night. One place I liked once was perfect, right up until 2.pm when all the kids came out of school at the end of the street and the mums would block all the drives with their cars waiting to pick them up, every day just imagine that.

If there are bars or hotels near then you must go to that area at night, as things can be very different around a property at night with parking and noise.

Another Top tip would be only getting recommended people that you have personally seen what they can do. Go see work that people have done and ask clients what they thought as any good worker will be happy for you to do this.

They may well be lovely people when you speak to them but what's their work like? as that's what you will be paying for. At the builders merchants you can ask them for trade's people that they know and recommend. They normally have a book of draw full of their business cards. Always get 3 different trades people to quote you to compare.

Then get a good architect that you like and who is on the same wave length as you on what and how you want to build your own house, make sure he knows how the process works as not all of them do.

Don't ever push council officers to get things done faster, it only alienates them, it takes a long time here sometimes a really long time and almost all paperwork here is in triplicate when it comes to building a new house.

When at these council or government offices try and be as friendly to staff as possible, most times builders or architects that present these plans and papers are very cold. Try and ask that person's name and ask how the system works, some are pretty friendly if you are and that may help later if you need to go back to see them.

Get a project manager for a few days every week unless you really know what you are doing, as paying for one can save you money in the long run and shields you some from stress.

The trailer we bought was a great help and I would recommend getting one.

A trailer was a great idea and mine cost 1200 euros new and was designed just for me as I wanted it. Even now I use it almost every week, most trailers fit on a normal car and they can save you money on deliveries. Buy new if you can as it will get used a lot and you don't need any problems. Know just what weight you can carry as fines are high if you over load it.

Buy some dummy security cameras and place them where you can. I had 2 and put a false wire coming out of them to make them look real. Some have the battery blinking light. These are cheap about 10 euros on Amazon and very realistic and can put thieves off.

You are going to be having expensive equipment and tools everywhere so this I feel a great idea.

Your local builder's stores sometimes have trades people selling off second hand tools or they know where you can buy tools cheaper so also ask. Personally I bought a few things this way and saved money. Some tools don't need to be in great condition.

Fencing off your new plot is very important and needs to be done as soon as you are the owner of it.

Make sure you fence off the land ASAP as you are responsible, even if there's nothing on the land. If someone walks their dog on your land and they fall over they can sue you, so get it fenced off ASAP.

We also had chains on the gates. You could have pushed the gates over if you really wanted to but the chains and locks just make it look more secure.

I also had a solar powered security light that was I think a good idea.

I bought the 2m by 3m mess that you can later put in the ground to reinforce the cement, so saving money as it gets used twice. My Spanish friend who's starting her build paid 3500 to have a nice chain link fence that they will dump once the house is finished as it's no good to anyone after.

Live near the house build or on it if possible as this also saves time and money.

If you contract anyone always get it in writing just what they will do and the cost including everything, even 2 extra power points we needed here after cost us another 200 euros when we thought they were included.

Always go over the top in asking is it all included, because you or they will always forget something and that can cost you in the end.

Also arrange a payment time table so you and they know just when you need to pay them. Most do weekly here or at each stage of the works so you need something in writing as many trades have other jobs on the go and yours may not always be the most important to them. If they know they need to finish stages to get their next payment that will encourage them more to stay on your site.

One of my neighbours had a lot of problems with a worker who said he needed payment to continue the works and they fell out and then he had to employ a new guy to go over what was done so paid twice in the end.

Make lists.

Making lists is very important, like lists of what you think you will need and the costs next to it, then keep adding to these lists when you are out and see what things you need and what they cost. You will become a price expert in time and know where the best prices have and this is a good thing.

Personally I made daily list of what I thought I could do each day, just rough lists as a guide for me but these really helped keep me focused on what was more important. Even down to what I needed to do in the mornings and then what I was planning to do in the afternoons. These lists after a few days became more detailed and did help me get things done faster.

Also I did a works list and time scale for me and with the help of my architect one for the workers. They normally have a time table of works but it's nice to see each week just were you are.

Have folders of quotes and a log book with all the phone numbers and keep all factoras for everything you buy, even the small things.

When buying materials try and buy in bulk or several things at the same time in the same place to get bigger discounts or at least free delivery.

Most of our kitchen appliances I put on the trailer and this not only saved time and delivery costs but a few things had no packaging so where cheaper but still with all the same guarantees.

Time management is also the key, so if you made lists of things you need to go buy then think about that trip and what shops you need to go to and what's really important to get and what's not.

Builder's stores are always busy first few hours in the mornings and straight after lunch so avoiding these times will save you loads. Monday morning first thing is never a good time as the world and his wife will be at these places and your wait ages.

I bought a bottle of cheap wine and gave it to the guy fetching the timber at a timber yard once, just a few weeks before Christmas and said thanks for your help. He was really shocked. It cost me 2.euros and every time I went there after that I have VIP treatment, even jumping the que many times and even got the old length of timer thrown in my trailer by accident.

Chapter 16

Links to companies and trades

First off here is the link to my **dream house build** blog that has videos, links and costs.

http://britishexpatsinspain.com/davids-dream-house-in-spain

David's books   https://livinginspainbooks.com

David's blog
https://wordpress.com/view/britishexpatsinspain.com

David's Podcast show

 https://www.spreaker.com/show/living-in-spain-with-david-wright

David's YouTube channel
https://www.youtube.com/c/DavidWrightBritishExpatsInSpain

The pc program I used to design my house and many other smaller projects…. https://www.sketchup.com/

If you open a new email account you get 30 days free use so you can open a new email and do this every 30 days. Personally I upgraded to the basic and that was more than enough and very useful.

More design apps I have used here

 https://fakeclients.com/blog/the-best-graphic-design-apps

Leroy Merlin   https://www.leroymerlin.es

Remember to ask about the pro card and they can also recommend local trades people in your area.

Timber yards, Search in your area for the industrial estates where they load from   http://serreriaalmeriense.es

Kitchen and bathroom stores in all areas
https://emiliohernandez.com

Artificial grass, branches everywhere

https://realturf.com/en/where-buy/artificial-turf-almeria

Planning registry officer where you can ask for free about any property just go to your local town hall and ask there.

Best skip hire is through your local builders merchants where they have sand and cement, they will also include the license you normally need to have and remember to get receipts as you will need these later when you need to show where you dumped the rubbish.

Water supply connections in Spain
https://www.aqualia.com/es/

Electric supply in Spain   https://www.endesa.com/es

Internet is important and we had ours connected even before we had any walls up and they put it temporally in the garage. We use movie star and they were very good connecting us with fibre optic.

If you are in Almeria area and would like trades people that I have used then connect with me through my blog of Facebook group, I am happy to give you numbers of trade's people I have used in my area.

Contact David https://britishexpatsinspain.com/

If you are looking for information on **moving to Spain** or **Finding work in Spain** then remember that I have 2 more books out on Amazon and Kindle that may be free to download on some devices.

See here https://livinginspainbooks.com/

This is not the end of this book as it will be updated and new info added in the future as it's a digital book on Amazon.

If you have the paperback or hard copy then just contact me through my sites and send me a photo of you holding a copy that you have bought and I will send you the link to a private website of mine where all my book updates are and you can access them all for <u>free for ever</u> with the password I will send you.

If you have a dream, whatever that dreams is, then you owe it to yourself to go after that dream with all your energy.

There's one saying I love....

Would you rather be sitting in a rest home at 80 years old in the cold UK watching repeats on TV saying "I wish I had done that"

OR

Sitting on your terrace in the warm sun with a glass of wine saying "I am so dlad I did this"

So was it all worth it?

Hell yes we love our new house

Others will tell you that your crazy, stupid of just dreaming but remember that it's your dream not theirs.

Don't ever get put off going after what you want.

I still remember 19 years ago at my leaving party in England when a so called friend said that I would not last 2 years and that I would soon be back. That guy is still living in the same place and working at the same works and moaning about it all.

I am just a normal carpenter from Brighton who has struggled with dyslexia and left school with no qualifications at all.

So if I can do it then so can you.

Thank you for buying this book and I hope it has helped give you some valuable tips and advice. You can always react out to me on my sites or blog and I will be happy to help answer any questions I can. If I don't have the answers I am sure I know a man who does.

Remember if you give it a nice review on Amazon you will automatically be added to the party invite at my house this summer.

THE END

Printed in Great Britain
by Amazon